FOOD *from the* SUN
HOW PLANTS LIVE AND GROW

Harriet Brown

Rourke
Publishing LLC
Vero Beach, Florida 32964

www.rourkepublishing.com

PHOTO CREDITS: p. 17: Sally Bensusen/Science Photo Library; p. 26: Jonathan S. Blair/
Getty Images; p. 33: Vera Bogaerts/istockphoto.com; p. 27, 34: Nigel Cattlin/FLPA; p. 4:
Elena Elisseeva/istockphoto.com; pp. title page, 19, 36: Chris Fairclough/CFWImages.com;
p. 13 both: Chris Fairclough/Discovery Picture Library; p. 30: Foto Natura Stock/FLPA;
p. 39: Joe Gough/istockphoto.com; p. 10: Paul Gsell/istockphoto.com; p. 8, 15, 41:
istockphoto.com; p. 16: Silvia Jansen/istockphoto.com; p. 21: Chee-Onn Leong/
istockphoto.com; p. 9: Brenda McEwan/istockphoto.com; p. 29: Dave Michaels/Corbis;
p. 38: Neil Nathan/istockphoto.com; p. 12: David Nunuk/Science Photo Library; pp. 42,
43: Ed Parker/EASI-Images/CFWImages.com; p. 31: Susanna Pershern/istockphoto.com;
p. 23, both, 24: Photodisc; p. 7: Corey Rich/Aurora/Getty Images; p. 37: Rey Rojo/
CFWImages.com; pp. 34, 35 bottom: Malcolm Romain/istockphoto.com; p. 35 top: Yali Shi/
istockphoto.com; p. 18: Stephen Strathdee/istockphoto.com; p. 25: Herbert Zetti/Zefa/Corbis.

Cover picture shows the early green shoots of a plant. [istockphoto.com]

Produced for Rourke Publishing by Discovery Books
Editors: Geoff Barker, Amy Bauman, Rebecca Hunter
Designer: Ian Winton
Cover designer: Keith Williams
Illustrator: Stefan Chabluk
Photo researcher: Rachel Tisdale

Library of Congress Cataloging-in-Publication Data

Brown, Harriet.
   Food from the sun : how plants live and grow / Harriet Brown.
      p. cm. -- (Let's explore science)
   Includes index.
   ISBN 978-1-60044-600-9
   1. Photosynthesis--Juvenile literature. 2. Plants--Juvenile literature. I. Title.
   QK882.B83 2008
   572'.46--dc22
                                 2007019958

Printed in the USA

CONTENTS

CHAPTER ONE
GETTING STARTED

The Sun is the source for all life on Earth. It gives out huge amounts of **energy** as light and heat. This energy travels across space to Earth. Here it is used by both plants and animals.

Plants, in particular, make good use of sunlight. A plant's leaves trap the energy from the Sun. They use it to make food. Plants in turn supply animals with food. Some animals eat the plants. Some eat the animals that eat the plants. In the end, all living things depend on the food from the Sun.

A tree's leaves are arranged to catch as much sunlight as possible.

What is Photosynthesis?

Photosynthesis is how plants make food from sunlight. It begins with the water and carbon dioxide that plants take in. With the energy from the Sun, plants turn these into simple sugars, called glucose. Oxygen is also created. Some of this is given off into the air that we breathe.

Where Does Photosynthesis Happen?

Photosynthesis happens in a plant's green leaves. Leaves look green because they contain a coloring matter, called **chlorophyll**. It is the chlorophyll that absorbs the sunlight.

Chloroplasts in the leaves contain chlorophyll. Chlorophyll traps the Sun's energy.

Photosynthesis

Oxygen out

Light energy

Chloroplasts

Carbon dioxide in

Water

The photosynthesis equation is:

Sunlight and Chlorophyll

Carbon dioxide + Water ➡ Glucose + Oxygen

FLYING TO THE SUN

The Sun is about 93 million miles (149.5 million kilometers) from Earth. Can you imagine how far away that is? Say that you could fly to the Sun in an airplane. It would take you over twenty-one years to get

Plant Cells

Photosynthesis happens in a plant's cells. The cells are tiny. You need a microscope to see them.

There are many types of plant cells. Each has a different job. But each has similar parts. One, the nucleus, controls what happens in the cell. The vacuole keeps the cell strong and rigid. Chloroplasts contain chlorophyll. This is where photosynthesis takes place. All of these parts sit in a jellylike matter called cytoplasm. These are protected by a cell **membrane**. Each plant cell also has a tough outer cell wall.

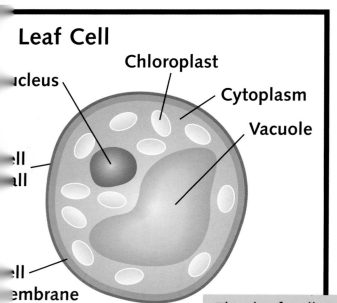

Leaf Cell

Nucleus

Chloroplast

Cytoplasm

Vacuole

Cell wall

Cell membrane

This leaf cell contains all of the structures it needs to carry out photosynthesis.

Respiration

Plants turn glucose into energy. This process is called respiration. They need the energy to live and grow. Plants only carry out photosynthesis when there is sunlight. Respiration happens all of the time. Inside the cells, plants use oxygen to turn glucose into energy. They also produce carbon dioxide and water.

The respiration equation is:

Glucose + Oxygen $\longrightarrow$ Carbon dioxide + Water + Energy

Starch

On a sunny day, plants make lots of glucose. This lasts them through the night and through several cloudy days. But they cannot store up lots of glucose. Glucose that isn't used in respiration is turned into starch. Starch can be stored in leaf cells for later use.

In bright sunshine, you can be sure that green plants are making lots of glucose.

Why Do Plants Need Energy?

All living things carry out the seven life processes.
They need energy for these processes. They include:

- **M**ovement: Plants move their leaves to face the Sun.
- **R**espiration: Plants turn glucose into energy.
- **S**ensitivity: Plants react to their surroundings.
- **G**rowth: Plants grow from a seed to full plant.
- **R**eproduction: Plants have offspring.
- **E**xcretion: Plants get rid of waste.
- **N**utrition: Plants make their own food.

Look at the first letter of each process. Together, they form the words "MRS GREN." This will help you remember the seven life processes.

This plant has pushed through the soil toward the Sun as it grows.

IN THE DARK

Some plants need darkness. Plants called poinsettias need twelve hours of darkness each day. They do not flower if there is too much light. Other plants are even more sensitive to light. If the night is interrupted by a blink of light, they will not flower.

Pale Plants

Plants need sunlight to grow properly. Stems hold the leaves so that they face sunlight. But sometimes, there is very little sunlight. Then, the stems grow longer as they try to find light. They may be weak and spindly. The leaves turn pale. The plants will die unless they get sunlight.

CHAPTER TWO
WATER FOR LIFE

Plants are 90 percent water. They need water for photosynthesis to take place. If plants do not get enough water, photosynthesis slows down. Water also keeps a plant's leaves and stems from drooping.

The leaves of pond plants spread out on the water's surface. The roots beneath them can get plenty of water.

Water Storage

Plants store water in sacs, called vacuoles, in their cells. When the vacuole is full of water, the cells are rigid and firm. The vacuole pushes out on the cell membrane and cell wall. The cells are said to be **turgid**. Sometimes, there is not much water in the vacuole. Then, the cells become soft and floppy. The vacuole no longer pushes on the cell membrane and wall. Then, cells are described as **flaccid**.

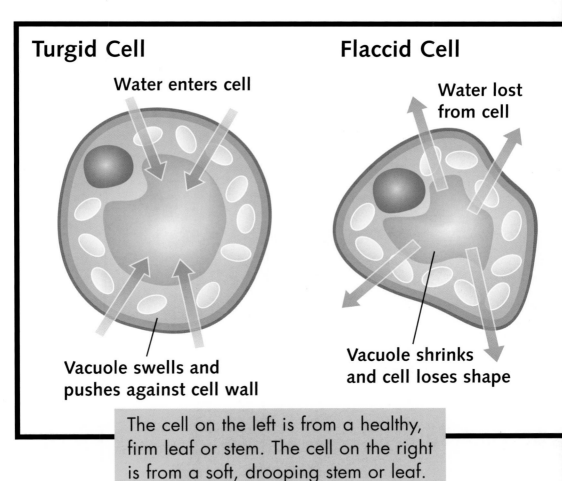

Turgid Cell

Water enters cell

Vacuole swells and pushes against cell wall

Flaccid Cell

Water lost from cell

Vacuole shrinks and cell loses shape

The cell on the left is from a healthy, firm leaf or stem. The cell on the right is from a soft, drooping stem or leaf.

When the cells are turgid, the stems are strong and straight. The leaves are fully open and spread out. The leaves have a large flat area that can catch lots of sunlight. The more turgid the leaf cells, the more photosynthesis can take place.

How Do Plants Get Water?

Plants have roots. They anchor the plants in the ground. The roots are surrounded by soil. Water moves from the soil into the plants' roots. This happens by **osmosis**. In osmosis, water moves from an area with lots of water to an area where there is less. This usually happens across a membrane. The membrane chooses what can cross it and what can not cross it.

The roots of these plants spread out. This way they can reach as much water as possible.

At the end of a plant's root is a mass of tiny root hairs. Root hairs are cells. They increase the **surface area** of the root. The bigger the surface area, the more water can cross into the plant.

Water travels through the roots, up the stems, and into the leaves. You can see this for yourself in this experiment. Cut the bottom off a stick of celery. Put it into a jar of water. Add food coloring to the water. Let it sit for a day. Take out the celery and cut the stem again. Look at the cut surface. You will see dots of color. That means the water is moving up the stem.

You can try the same experiment using a white flower (above). The petals should change color (right).

How Do Plants Lose Water?

Plants lose water through tiny holes on the bottom of their leaves. The holes are much smaller than a pinhead. You need a microsope to see these, too. The holes are called **stomata**. Water vapor moves out of the leaves through the stomata. This is called **evaporation**.

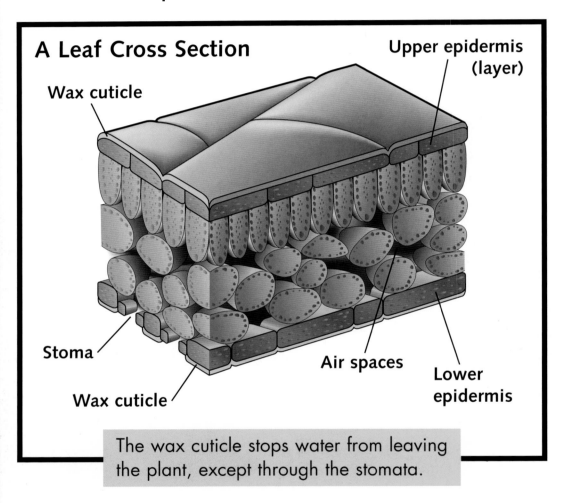

A Leaf Cross Section

Upper epidermis (layer)

Wax cuticle

Stoma

Air spaces

Wax cuticle

Lower epidermis

The wax cuticle stops water from leaving the plant, except through the stomata.

Plants open the stomata to let in carbon dioxide for photosynthesis. At the same time, water moves out.

Weather conditions affect how much water plants lose. For example, a plant will lose more water in a hot desert than it would at the North Pole.

Weather Condition	Water Loss	Why?
Hot day	More water loss	Heat makes water evaporate faster.
Cold day	Less water loss	Less heat means less evaporation.
Windy day	More water loss	Wind blows evaporated water from the plant. This allows more water to evaporate.
Calm day	Less water loss	Less wind means that evaporated water stays near the plant. This stops more water from evaporating.
Low **humidity** (air containing less water vapor)	More water loss	Air with low humidity does not hold much water. There is plenty of space for extra water to evaporate from the plant.
High humidity (air containing more water vapor)	Less water loss	Humid air is full of water. This stops more water from evaporating.

A LOT OF WATER

In a year, an oak tree can lose 40,000 gallons (151,000 liters) of water from its leaves. This is a lot of water. Imagine this. You would use the same amount of water if you stood in a shower for almost a week.

CHAPTER THREE
SOIL FOR LIFE

Plants make most of their food by photosynthesis. But they also need **minerals** to be healthy. Plants cannot make minerals. They get them from the soil. Some of the minerals they need include the following:

Nitrates

Nitrates provide nitrogen. Nitrogen helps plants grow. All living cells contain nitrogen. Nitrogen is also part of chlorophyll, the **pigment** that traps sunlight. No nitrogen means no photosynthesis. You can tell if a plant does not have enough nitrogen. It will be small. Its older leaves will be yellow.

armers spray fertilizers onto their crops. The fertilizers usually contain nitrates.

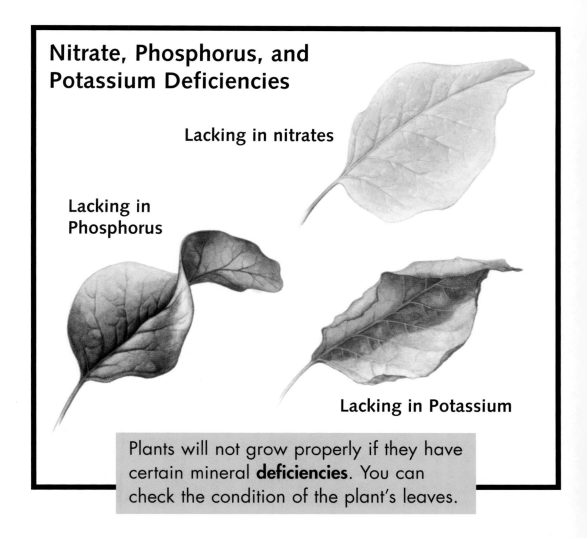

Nitrate, Phosphorus, and Potassium Deficiencies

Lacking in nitrates

Lacking in Phosphorus

Lacking in Potassium

Plants will not grow properly if they have certain mineral **deficiencies**. You can check the condition of the plant's leaves.

Phosphorus

Phosphorus is important for photosynthesis, respiration, and growth. It encourages roots to grow well. You can tell if a plant does not have enough phosphorus. Its roots will be stunted. Its younger leaves will be purple.

Potassium

Potassium helps chemicals called enzymes to work. Enzymes are needed in photosynthesis and respiration. Potassium can also protect a plant from disease. You can tell if a plant does not have enough potassium. Its leaves will be yellow. They will have dead parts on them.

The soil in this field has been overused by a farmer. Crops may not grow well here unless the farmer adds fertilizer.

How Do Plants Obtain Minerals?

Plants get water through their roots. This is how they get minerals, too. From the roots, the minerals travel to the stems and leaves.

When plants die, the minerals go back to the soil. This keeps the soil rich. But sometimes a plant is part of a crop. Then it will be harvested by a farmer. This means that the minerals won't go back to the soil. Eventually, the soil is **exhausted** of minerals.

Helping Soil and Plants

But minerals can be added to soil to make it rich again. This can be done with fertilizers. Fertilizers can be natural or human-made. Natural fertilizers include manure, seaweed, and rock powders. Human-made fertilizers are mixtures of chemicals.

Soil can also be improved by resting the land. The farmer does not grow any crops on a piece of land for a year. Or, different crops can be grown on the land in different years. Both ideas can repair the damaged soil.

ORGANIC FERTILIZERS

Some people will not eat plants that have been grown using artificial fertilizers. They think it is unhealthy. They eat only plants grown without any human-made chemicals. These plants are called organic.

These people are harvesting seaweed. They will use it as a fertilizer for plants.

CHAPTER FOUR

PLANT TRANSPORT

Plants have tubes that run through their stems and roots. These tubes carry water, minerals, and sugars. There are two types of tubes: **xylem** and **phloem**. The xylem and phloem connect the top and bottom of the plant. Each has its own job.

Xylem

Xylem are strong, thick tubes. They carry water and minerals from the plant's roots to its leaves. Water and minerals must reach the leaves. There they will be available for use in photosynthesis.

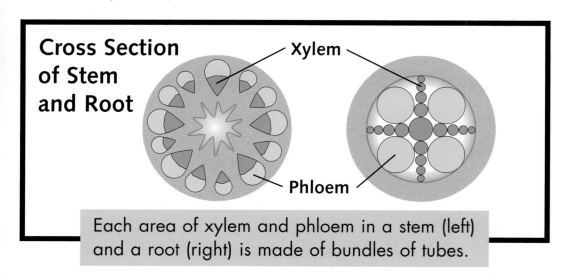

Cross Section of Stem and Root

Xylem

Phloem

Each area of xylem and phloem in a stem (left) and a root (right) is made of bundles of tubes.

Phloem

Phloem are thinner tubes than xylem. They carry the glucose made in photosynthesis. They move the glucose from the leaves to wherever it is needed in the plant's body. The glucose can be used to produce energy in respiration. It also can be stored as starch.

Roots and Stems

The xylem and phloem are arranged differently in roots and stems. Together, they make up the **vascular tissue**.

Even in a huge tree like this one, the xylem must carry water all the way from the roots to the leaves at the top.

CHAPTER FIVE

REPRODUCTION

Flowers come in many shapes, colors, and sizes. They are a plant's reproductive organs. They usually contain both male and female sex organs. Some major parts are shown below.

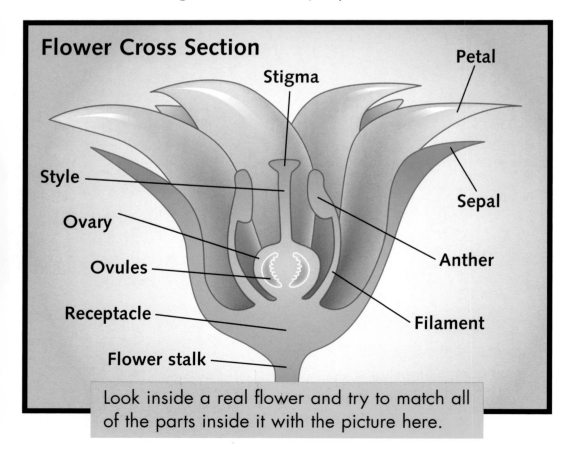

Flower Cross Section

Stigma

Petal

Style

Sepal

Ovary

Ovules

Anther

Receptacle

Filament

Flower stalk

Look inside a real flower and try to match all of the parts inside it with the picture here.

Not all flowers look the same, but most of them contain the same parts. It is harder to find each part in a plant like this though!

Stamen

The **stamen** is a male part. It is made up of long stalks, called filaments. At the top of the long filament is the anther. The anther produces pollen. The pollen contains the male sex cell.

Carpel

The **carpel** is a female part of the flower. It has a wide ovary at its base. This leads up into a narrow style. At the top of the style is a sticky stigma. Eggs are produced in the ovary. Eggs are the female sex cells.

Petals

Some plants have brightly colored petals. These attract insects and birds. (See page 24.)

Sepals

Sepals are leafy parts. They are found at the bottom of the flower. When the flower is a bud, the sepals wrap around it. This protects the flower inside while it develops.

Daisies are common flowers in many parts of the world. Compare a daisy bud with an open daisy flower. See if you can find the sepals in each one.

What Is Pollination?

Pollination is the movement of pollen from the anther to the stigma. This is how plants reproduce. For a plant to reproduce, the pollen and the egg must meet. It is best if they come from different plants. This makes sure the offspring are strong and healthy.

Animal-Pollinated Plants

Some plants are pollinated by animals. These plants have brightly colored petals. They also have sweet-smelling nectar. The color and smell attract birds, insects, and some animals to the flower. They feed on the nectar. They move into the flower to reach the nectar. Pollen brushes onto their bodies. Next they move off to feed from another flower. They carry the pollen with them. The pollen brushes off onto the stigma of another plant.

Butterflies can see well. They are attracted to brightly colored petals, especially red petals.

This bee is completely covered in yellow, sticky pollen.

Wind-Pollinated Plants

Other plants are pollinated by the wind. These plants have long stamens. The stamens hang outside of the flower. Wind blows the pollen off the anthers. The pollen blows around in the air. Some of the pollen will eventually be carried to the stigma of another plant.

What Are the Differences Between Animal- and Wind-Pollinated Plants?

This table shows the main differences:

Animal-Pollinated Plants	Wind-Pollinated Plants
Pollen is sticky and heavy.	Pollen is smooth and light.
Petals are brightly colored.	Petals may be dull or not present at all.
Stamens are inside the flower.	Stamens hang outside the flower.

Not only insects feed from flowers. These Australian honey possums are feeding from this flower. They may transfer pollen to the next flower they visit.

This hazel tree is wind pollinated. You can see the pollen blowing around in the wind.

What is Fertilization?

Once the pollen lands on the stigma, it must find the eggs. The pollen grows a tube. The tube travels down the style and into the ovary. The ovary contains the eggs. Part of the pollen travels down the tube to the eggs. When the male pollen and the female egg meet, **fertilization** takes place. Fertilization is the joining of the pollen and the egg. Fertilization forms a seed. Seeds contain everything they need to grow into a new plant.

LONG-TONGUED BATS

Bats can pollinate flowers, too. They drink the sugary nectar and eat pollen. The tube lipped bat, from Ecuador, has a record-breaking tongue. It can extend its tongue to 1.5 times its body length. This helps the bat reach into trumpet-shaped flowers. Imagine your tongue were that long. It would be over six feet (2 m) long!

CHAPTER SIX
ALL ABOUT SEEDS

After the seeds have formed, the petals drop off. The flower dies. The ovary becomes a fruit. The seeds are inside the fruit. Some fruits can be soft and juicy. Others are hard and tough. The flesh of an apple is the ovary. Nuts have hard, tough ovaries. Sometimes, seeds do not form inside fruits. Strawberries have seeds covering the outside.

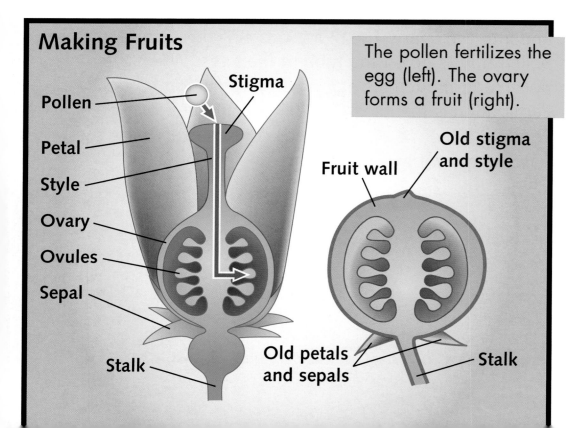

Making Fruits

The pollen fertilizes the egg (left). The ovary forms a fruit (right).

Pollen

Stigma

Petal

Style

Ovary

Ovules

Sepal

Stalk

Fruit wall

Old stigma and style

Old petals and sepals

Stalk

How Do Seeds Find a Good Place to Grow?

Plants spread their seeds. This is called seed **dispersal**. There are four main ways that plants do this.

1. Wind Dispersal

You may have seen sycamore seeds spinning in the air. Or maybe you have seen dandelion seeds blowing in the breeze. These seeds are moving away from their parent plants. Sycamore seeds have a "wing." When they fall from a tree, they spin in circles. This helps them stay in the air longer than if they fell straight down.

A breeze or wind can blow the seeds. They will land far from the parent tree. Dandelion seeds are very light. They easily carry a long way on a breeze.

Each dandelion seed has a fluffy parachute. The parachute carries the seed in the air far from the parent plant.

2. Animal Dispersal

Many people enjoy seeds and nuts. Animals and birds enjoy seeds and nuts, too. Seeds have a tough outer coat. When an animal eats a seed, the tough coat protects the seed. The seed does not break down in the animal's stomach. Instead, it passes out in the animal's waste. This helps it travel a long way from the parent plant.

Other seeds are sticky. Some have hooks on their surfaces. When an animal brushes past the plant, the seeds cling to the animal's fur. Eventually, the animal cleans its fur. The seed falls off.

This seed is hooked onto a mammal's fur. Eventually it will drop off and it may grow into a new plant.

This coconut seed is sprouting into a new tree. It will grow roots and a long trunk. One day it may produce its own seeds.

3. Water Dispersal

Coconuts are huge seeds. They are seeds that float on water. If coconuts fall on a beach, the sea may carry them away. They can survive in the water for many weeks. Eventually, they might wash up on another beach. There they can grow into a new coconut tree.

SLEEPY SEEDS

Seeds must have the right conditions to grow into a new plant. Until the do, they can lie inactive, or dormant, for many years. Being dormant is lik being in a long sleep.

This Himalayan balsam plant forms pods. When the pod dries, the seeds get flung out far and wide.

4. Self Dispersal

Some plants have clever ways to disperse their seeds. They do not need animals, water, or the wind. Peas form inside a pea pod. When the pod dries up, the peas are flung out. This is like a tiny explosion.

Why Does the Seed Move Away?

If a seed grows next to its parent plant, it may not grow very well. Both plants need energy from the Sun. If they are too close together, they could shade each other from the Sun. They both also need minerals from the soil. They could end up fighting each other for food and light.

ANCIENT DATES

Seeds can survive a long time. The oldest seed ever to grow into a plant was two thousand years old. It was a date palm. The date palm seed survived buried in the ground near the Dead Sea in Israel. Scientists thought that this type of date palm was extinct. Luckily, they were wrong!

How Does a New Plant Grow?

If a seed is lucky, it will land on good soil. When the conditions are right, it may grow into a new plant. This is called **germination**. Seeds contain their own energy store. They do not need light at first. But they do need water, warm temperatures, and oxygen.

If a seed has the right conditions, it grows a root. The root pushes down into the soil. Then it grows a shoot. The shoot pushes up through the soil. When it reaches the air, its new leaves uncurl. At this point, the seed can use its leaves to trap energy from the Sun. It does not need its own energy store any more. Now, it carries out photosynthesis. This will help it grow into a strong, full-grown plant.

Germination

1. The root grows down. A shoot begins to grow.

2. The shoot develops and reaches toward the light.

1   2

The growth stages of a seed—from young roots and shoot to a long stem and leaves.

This crop of rice is sprouting. As soon as the green leaves develop, photosynthesis starts to take place.

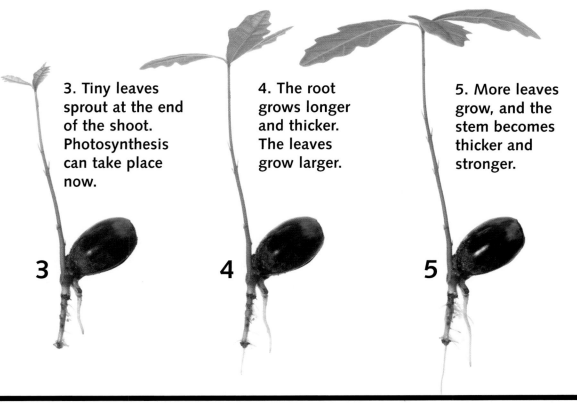

3. Tiny leaves sprout at the end of the shoot. Photosynthesis can take place now.

4. The root grows longer and thicker. The leaves grow larger.

5. More leaves grow, and the stem becomes thicker and stronger.

CHAPTER SEVEN
PLANT SURVIVAL

Our planet has about 260,000 species, or types, of plants. They are found all over the place: your backyard, the rainforests, the deserts, and the poles.

Plants cannot move from place to place the way animals can. That is why it is important that they are in the right environment. For example, a cactus would not grow very well at the South Pole.

Sunflowers only grow well where the weather is warm and sunny. They turn their flowers to face the Sun.

How Do Plants Adapt?

Some plants move every day. They turn their leaves toward the Sun. Sunflower plants turn toward the Sun. They do this to catch as much sunlight as possible.

When a fern sprouts, its leaves are curled up tightly. Next, the leaves uncurl and begin to photosynthesize.

Other plants adapt according to the season. In a woodland, lots of plants compete for light. In spring, plants grow new leaves. Ferns are one of the first plants to grow new leaves. They do this before the trees have sprouted leaves. This way, they can catch lots of light before they are shaded by the trees.

In cold and exposed places, plants grow close to the ground so that they are protected from strong winds. There is not enough warmth or sunlight for them to grow tall.

How Do Plants Survive Extreme Conditions?

Each environment presents new problems for plants.

Deserts

Desert plants have plenty of sunlight. But they receive very little water. When it does rain, they soak up as much water as they can. Their roots are often very close to the surface of the soil or sand. They are ready and waiting to catch any drop of water that falls.

Their next challenge is to hang onto the water. Desert plants have a thick, waxy surface. They have spikes instead of leaves. This stops a lot of water from being lost across their outside surface.

Rainforests

Rainforests are found in hot, rainy regions of the world. They have a lot of sunlight and a lot of rain. Thousands of plant species grow here. They all compete for light and minerals. Rainforest trees grow very fast and extremely tall. Some stand over 150 feet (46 meters). The tallest trees get the most sunlight. In this way, they compete with each other for survival.

THE TALLEST TREES

Trees in a rainforest can be very tall. The tallest can grow to 300 feet (90 m) tall. That's about the same height as fifty men standing on each others' shoulders.

Dense rainforest in Australia is home to a massive variety of plants and animals.

CHAPTER EIGHT

PLANTS AND OUR PLANET

Around planet Earth is a layer of gases. This is the **atmosphere**. It contains nitrogen, oxygen, and carbon dioxide. The carbon dioxide acts like a blanket. It traps the Sun's heat. This is the natural **greenhouse effect**. We need this to survive on Earth.

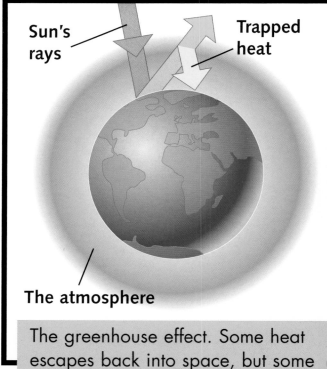

The greenhouse effect. Some heat escapes back into space, but some is trapped in the atmosphere.

What is Global Warming?

Among Earth's resources are the "fossil fuels." These include oil, natural gas, and coal. We burn fossil fuels in cars, factories, and airplanes. We burn it in power plants that make electricity. This produces carbon dioxide. The carbon dioxide goes into the atmosphere.

Factories release greenhouse gases into the air. This is causing global warming.

Today, there is too much carbon dioxide in the atmosphere. It is trapping too much heat. This causes our planet to warm up. This is global warming.

What is Climate Change?

Our climate is changing because of global warming. The climate is the average weather in a particular place over a long period of time. For example, the climate of a desert is hot and dry. The climate of the North Pole is very cold. Global warming is heating up the Earth. This is changing the climates of planet Earth.

Why is Climate Change a Problem?

As Earth becomes warmer, ice at the North and South Poles will melt. This could flood huge areas of land. Warmer temperatures could kill many species of plants and animals. They may be unable to adapt quickly enough to the new conditions. Climate change may also cause more violent weather, such as hurricanes.

Climate change could mean that some plants will not grow as well in the new climate.

How Do Plants Affect Climate Change?

Plants carry out photosynthesis. Land and ocean plants take in carbon dioxide. They release oxygen. We need plants to take in carbon dioxide. This helps reduce global warming. It can help slow down climate change.

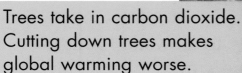

Trees take in carbon dioxide. Cutting down trees makes global warming worse.

What Can We Do?

Rainforests are being cut down. People use the wood for building. They use the cleared areas for cattle to graze. We need to protect the rainforests. This is a job for every one of us, and the governments of our world. If we all manage to save a little, this could make a huge difference to our planet.

GLOSSARY

atmosphere (AT muhss fihr) — the layer of gases that surrounds Earth

carpel (KAR puhl) — the female part of a flower

cell (sel) — the tiny structure from which all living things are made

chlorophyll (KLOR uh fil) — the green matter in plants

deficiency (di FISH uhn see) — lacking in something

dispersal (diss PURSS uhl) — when something spreads over an area

energy (EN uhr jee) — the ability to do work. Plants use energy from the Sun to live and grow.

evaporation (i VAP uh ray shuhn) — when a liquid turns into a gas or vapor

exhausted (eg ZAW sted) — completely empty of a substance or of energy

fertilization (FUR tuhl eye zay shuhn) — the joining of male and female cells. In plants, fertilization is when the pollen and egg meet and join.

flaccid (FLASS id) — limp, lacking in firmness

germination (JUR muh nay shuhn) — the sprouting of a new plant

greenhouse effect (GREEN houss uh FEKT) — the warming of Earth. The natural greenhouse effect is caused by carbon dioxide in the atmosphere keeping in heat from the Sun.

humidity (HYOO mid uh tee) — the measure of the amount of water in the air

membrane (MEM brayn) — a very thin skinlike sheet

mineral (MIN ur uhl) — a substance that occurs naturally in rocks and in the ground

osmosis (oz MOH siss) — the movement of a substance across a membrane (from where there is a lot of the substance to where there is less of it)

phloem (FLOH uhm) — plant tissue that carries food made by the plant to wherever it is needed

photosynthesis (foh toh SIN thuh siss) — the process by which plants use energy from the Sun, water, and carbon dioxide to make glucose and oxygen

pigment (PIG muhnt) — coloring substance

pollination (POL uh nay shuhn) — the transfer of pollen from the anther to the stigma of a plant

respiration (ress puh RAY shuhn) — the process in cells in which glucose and oxygen are used to produce energy, carbon dioxide, and water

stamen (STAY muhn) — the male part of a flower

stomata (STOH may ter) — the tiny pores (holes) on a plant's leaf

surface area (SUR fiss AIR ee uh) — the amount of space on the outside of an object

turgid (TUR jid) — swollen and firm

vascular tissue (VASS kyoo lur TISH oo) — the collection of plant tissues that move substances around the plant. This includes the xylem and the phloem.

xylem (ZYE luhm) — plant tissue that carries water and minerals from the roots all around the plant

FURTHER INFORMATION

Books
Photosynthesis And Respiration. William G. Hopkins.
   Chelsea House Publications, 2006.

Science with Plants. Helen Edom. Usborne Books, 2007.

Time for Kids: Plants! Editors of TIME for Kids.
   HarperTrophy, 2006.

*Understanding Photosynthesis With Max Axiom, Super
   Scientist*. Liam O'Donnell. Capstone Press, 2007.

Websites to visit
http://www.biology4kids.com/files/plants_main.html
   Information about the classification of plant types.
   Includes photosynthesis, structure, and reproduction.

http://www.urbanext.uiuc.edu/gpe/index.html
   The Great Plant Escape.
   Pick up your magnifying glass and help Detective Leplant
   solve many plant related mysteries!

**http://www.bbc.co.uk/schools/scienceclips/ages/9_10/
   life_cycles.shtml**
   This interactive site includes taking a flower apart by
   dragging and dropping each part into the relevant box.

http://www.naturegrid.org.uk/plant/index.html
Plant Explorer.
Click to find out what part of a plant a chip, a baked bean, or a cup of tea comes from.

http://www.sparta.k12.il.us/sid/plantunit/
Find out more about plants. Includes an in-depth look at the growth and life cycle of a bean plant.

INDEX